The Solar System

Steck Vaughn™

HOUGHTON MIFFLIN HARCOURT
Supplemental Publishers

www.SteckVaughn.com
800-531-5015

The Solar System

contents

The Solar System
Fact Matters

ISBN-13: 978-1-4190-5461-7
ISBN-10: 1-4190-5461-9

First published by Blake Education Pty Ltd as *Go Facts*
Copyright © 2006 Blake Publishing
This edition copyright under license from Blake Education Pty Ltd
© 2010 Steck-Vaughn, an imprint of HMH Supplemental Publishers Inc.

Printed in China

1 2 3 4 5 6 7 8   373   15 14 13 12 11 10 09 08

Our Solar System

The solar system is the Sun and all objects that **orbit** *it. These objects include the eight planets, their moons, asteroids, and comets.*

Circling the Sun

The Sun is a star. A star is a huge, spinning ball of hot gas. The Sun is the only star in our solar system. It provides light and heat to the planets. The Sun's **gravity** is the force that holds the solar system in place. It keeps the planets traveling around the Sun.

The Planets

Mercury, Venus, Earth, and Mars are the four planets closest to the Sun. They are rocky planets with metal cores. The next four planets are gas planets. They are Jupiter, Saturn, Uranus, and Neptune. They have rocky **cores**. These cores are covered by liquid or ice. These planets have layers of gas clouds on the outside.

Moons are rocky **satellites**. They orbit planets. Most planets have at least one moon. Mercury and Venus don't have any moons.

Asteroids are pieces of rock that orbit the Sun. Most asteroids are grouped together between Mars and Jupiter. Comets are made of ice, dust, and rock.

Pluto was considered the ninth planet in our solar system until 2006. It is now classified as a dwarf planet.

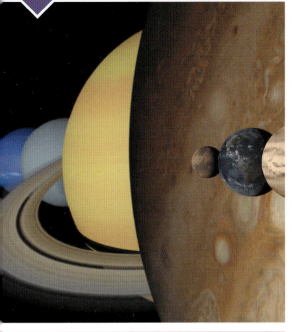

The solar system is part of the Milky Way galaxy. The Milky Way is a barred-spiral galaxy.

The inner solar system is separated from the outer by the asteroid belt.

Did You Know?

The Sun would still be more than 700 times bigger than all the planets joined together. It contains over 99 percent of the solar system's **mass**.

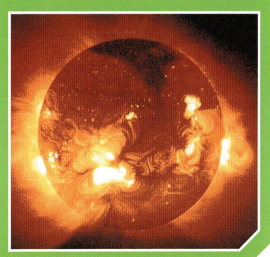

5

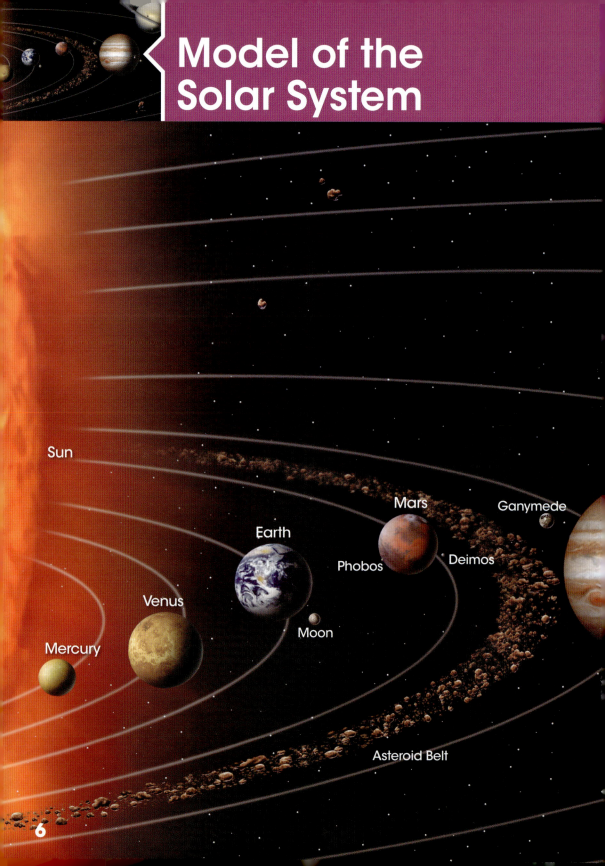

Model of the Solar System

Sun

Mercury

Venus

Earth

Moon

Mars

Phobos

Deimos

Ganymede

Asteroid Belt

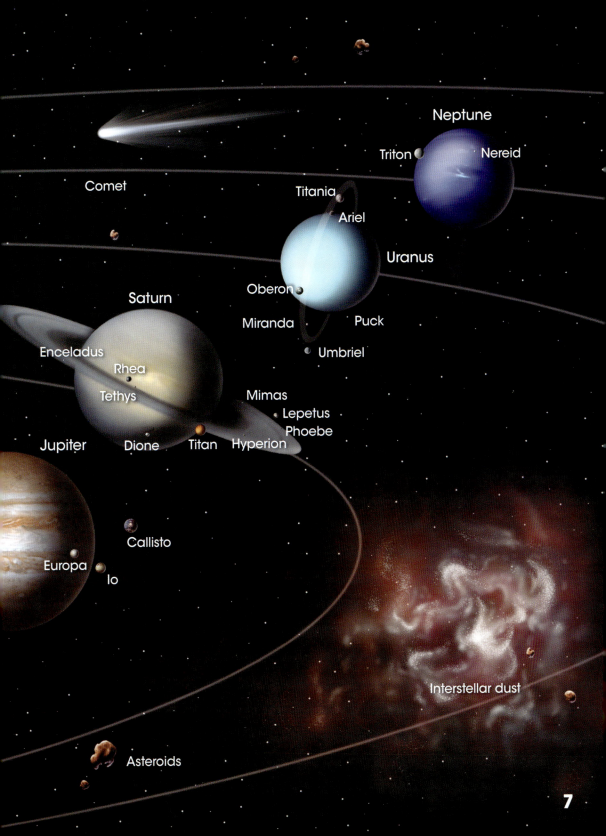

Neptune

Triton

Nereid

Comet

Titania

Ariel

Uranus

Saturn

Oberon

Enceladus

Miranda

Puck

Rhea

Umbriel

Tethys

Mimas

Lepetus

Phoebe

Jupiter

Dione

Titan

Hyperion

Callisto

Europa

Io

Interstellar dust

Asteroids

The Sun

The Sun is only an average-sized star. But the energy it produces allows life to exist on Earth.

Solar Energy

The Sun is a yellow **dwarf star**. Energy is produced in the Sun's core. This energy then travels to the outer part of the Sun. The high temperature and intense pressure create powerful **nuclear reactions** within the Sun's core. Atoms of hydrogen smash together. They fuse to form helium. This produces light and heat energy. The energy **radiates** outward to the **surface** of the Sun. The Sun's surface is called the photosphere.

The Speed of Light

Light and other **radiation** travel from the Sun's surface to other parts of the solar system. It takes 8 minutes and 17 seconds for this energy to reach Earth. Our planet is about 93 million miles away from the Sun.

The Sun's energy is essential for life on Earth. It provides light for plants to grow. Plants are the basis of all food chains. The Sun also provides heat. This heat creates our weather. The water cycle depends on this heat to bring about water evaporation. Water evaporation creates clouds and rain.

It takes two million years for **gamma rays** produced in the Sun's core to reach its surface.

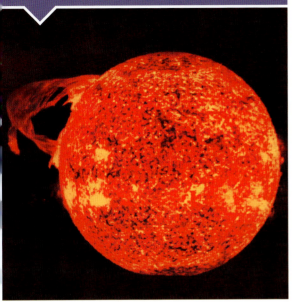

The Sun is the largest object in the solar system. It is about 332,950 times more massive than Earth.

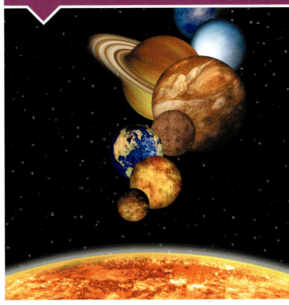

The relationship between the Sun and the Earth drives the seasons, ocean currents, weather, and climate.

Did You Know?

The Sun has been burning for about five billion years. It will burn for another five billion.

Mercury and Venus

Mercury and Venus are the two planets closest to the Sun. The conditions on each planet are very different.

Rocky Planets

Both Mercury and Venus are made of solid rock, but they look completely different. About 60 percent of Mercury's surface is covered by **craters**. These craters were caused by **meteorites** crashing into the planet. This makes it look very similar to Earth's moon. Venus has many volcanoes.

There is a major difference between the **atmospheres** on the two planets. Mercury has almost no atmosphere. Venus has a thick atmosphere of carbon dioxide. It is covered by spinning clouds of **sulfuric acid**.

Temperature

Although Mercury is the closest planet to the Sun, Venus is actually the hotter planet. Mercury's temperature can reach up to 800 degrees Fahrenheit during the day. The temperature can fall to around -300 degrees at night. This is because there is no atmosphere to trap heat near the surface of the planet. On Venus, any heat that finds its way through the thick atmosphere is trapped near the surface of the planet. This produces a **greenhouse effect**. The temperature reaches around 896 degrees Fahrenheit. This heat also means water cannot exist as a liquid on either Mercury or Venus.

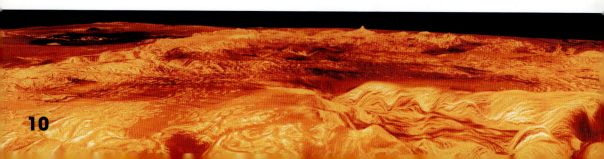

Much of the surface of Venus has been covered in lava from previous volcanic eruptions.

Mercury has the greatest variation in surface temperature of any planet in the solar system. This variation can be over 1,100 degrees Fahrenheit.

Mercury and Venus are the only two planets in our solar system that don't have moons.

The atmospheric pressure on Venus is the same as if you were about 3,000 feet underneath an ocean on Earth.

Earth and Its Moon

Earth is the only planet in our solar system with all the conditions needed for life to exist.

Earth is the only planet with a temperature that allows liquid water to exist. The other planets are either too close to the Sun or too far away. It is also the only planet to have an atmosphere that contains 21 percent oxygen, which we need to breathe, and 78 percent nitrogen. This atmosphere protects Earth from the Sun's **ultraviolet** rays. It also traps some of the Sun's heat and transports liquid around the planet in the form of rain.

Earth only has one natural satellite—the Moon. It is about one-quarter the size of Earth. It has no water, wind, air, or atmosphere. The Moon is held in orbit by Earth's gravity. We always see the same side of the Moon on Earth. This is because the Moon takes the same time to spin on its **axis** as it does to orbit the Earth. Although the Moon only has weak gravity, it is close enough to Earth to affect our oceans. It is the Moon that causes the rise and fall of our tides.

The official Latin name for Earth is *Terra*. It is named after a Roman goddess, Terra Mater.

Any footprints left on the Moon by astronauts should remain for millions of years. This is because there is no wind or rain on the Moon.

Many scientists believe that Earth was hit by a large object. The **debris** that was ejected into space joined to form the Moon.

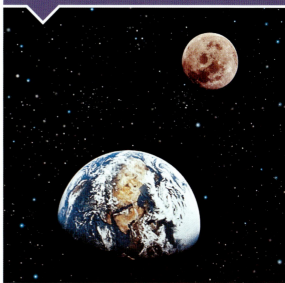

Did You Know?

The Moon is the only other planet or satellite in the solar system that humans have set foot upon.

Mars

Mars is a red planet with some similar features to Earth. It is still not known whether Mars has ever supported life.

Similar Features

The soil on Mars contains iron oxide. This gives the planet its red color. Iron oxide is a mineral also found in Earth's soil.

There is evidence that water once flowed on Mars. There are valleys that have been eroded by water. There are also dry riverbeds. Mars has icecaps at its north and south poles, like Earth.

The length of a Martian day is about 40 minutes longer than a day on Earth. Mars also has a similar tilt on its axis to Earth. It has the same pattern of seasons.

Volcanoes occur on Mars. Olympus Mons on Mars is the largest volcano in the solar system. It is about 15 miles high and 370 miles wide.

Cold with No Oxygen

There are significant differences between the atmospheres on Mars and on Earth. Mars has a very thin atmosphere of carbon dioxide. This means that we could not survive on Mars.

Mars is a very cold planet. The temperature falls to as low as -184 degrees Fahrenheit. The highest temperature is around 32 degrees. Winds on Mars can cause huge dust storms. These storms cover the whole planet.

The surface area of Mars is approximately equal to that of Earth's dry land because Mars does not have any oceans.

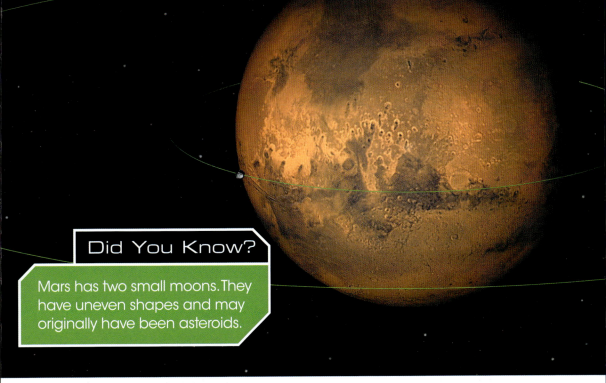

Did You Know?

Mars has two small moons. They have uneven shapes and may originally have been asteroids.

The length of each Martian season is almost twice as long as a season on Earth.

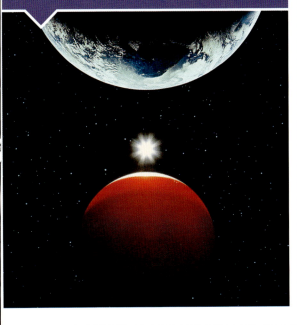

Mars has the least hostile environment of all the planets in the solar system.

Jupiter and Saturn

*Jupiter is the largest planet in the solar system. It has the fastest **rotation**. Saturn is the second largest planet. It is surrounded by rings of ice-covered rock. Both are gas giants.*

Jupiter

If all the other planets were combined into one planet, its mass would be less than half of Jupiter's. Jupiter is 317 times larger than Earth.

Jupiter completes its rotation in less than ten hours. This speed results in strong winds and huge cloud bands. Strong storms develop where these bands of clouds meet. One hurricane has existed for over 300 years. It is known as the Great Red Spot.

Saturn

Like Jupiter, Saturn is made of hydrogen and helium gas. Saturn's rotation is almost as fast as Jupiter's. Saturn also has very strong winds. They reach speeds that are 11 times faster than a hurricane on Earth.

There are thousands of rings surrounding Saturn. Each ring contains pieces of ice and rock traveling in orbit around Saturn. The rings closer to the planet seem to hold larger pieces. The outer rings contain finer materials.

Both Jupiter and Saturn have many satellites. Some were discovered very recently. Jupiter seems to have the most moons of any planet in our solar system. It has at least 62 moons. Saturn has more than 30.

Saturn is almost exactly the same as Jupiter, just smaller. The only striking difference is the rings around Saturn.

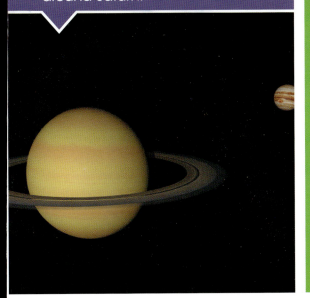

Jupiter is made of hydrogen and helium gases. These gases also make up the Sun. If Jupiter had been any bigger, it could have become a star.

Saturn's rings are thought to be particles of an old moon. This moon was smashed to pieces in a collision, millions of years ago.

Jupiter is usually the fourth brightest object in the sky, after the Sun, the Moon, and Venus.

17

Uranus, Neptune, and Pluto

The two farthest planets from the Sun are Uranus and Neptune. They are both gas planets.

Blue-Green Methane

Both Uranus and Neptune have atmospheres of hydrogen, helium, and methane. The methane gives these planets a blue-green color. Below the atmosphere, both planets have liquid layers of **water ice**, methane, and ammonia around rocky cores.

Uranus

Uranus, its rings, and moons all orbit the Sun. They are tipped on their sides. This may have been caused by a collision with another huge object. The result is that each pole on Uranus receives 42 Earth years of sunlight, followed by 42 years of darkness.

Neptune

Neptune, like Uranus, has rings and moons. It has a stormy atmosphere. Neptune has the fastest recorded winds in the solar system. These storms may be caused by heat generated within Neptune.

Pluto

Until 2006, Pluto was considered the ninth planet in our solar system. Pluto is now considered a dwarf planet. It is usually farthest away from the Sun. It takes 248 Earth years for Pluto to complete its **elliptical** orbit of the Sun. However, for 10 percent of its orbit, Pluto is closer to the Sun than Neptune. It has one large moon, Charon.

Neptune receives very little heat. This is because its orbit is so far from the Sun. The uppermost regions of its atmosphere are -360 degrees Fahrenheit.

It takes 84 Earth years for Uranus to complete one full orbit around the Sun.

Pluto may be an icy asteroid from the **Kuiper Belt**.

Did You Know?

Pluto and Charon have the same rotation period. This means the same side of Charon always faces the same side of Pluto.

Asteroids, Meteoroids, and Comets

Asteroids are pieces of rock and iron that orbit the Sun. Meteoroids are smaller bits of material that fly through space. Comets orbit the Sun. They are made of ice, dust, and rock.

Asteroids

Asteroids are known as minor planets. They range in size from a few meters across to more than 600 miles wide. The largest asteroid, Ceres, is almost 621 miles wide. Many asteroids are found orbiting in a belt between Mars and Jupiter.

Meteoroids

Meteoroids travel at great speeds. When they enter Earth's atmosphere, they burn up due to friction with the air. These streaks of light are called meteors, or shooting stars. Some meteors don't burn up completely because of their large size. They hit Earth's surface. These are called meteorites.

The Barrington Crater in Arizona was formed when a 100–160 foot iron meteorite hit Earth about 50,000 years ago. It is one of about 120 impact craters on Earth.

Comets

There are billions of comets orbiting the Sun. A comet doesn't have a tail for most of its orbit. A comet begins to warm up as it moves close to the Sun. Gas and dust from the nucleus begin to form a cloud or a coma around the nucleus. The Sun and its solar wind blow the coma into two tails. One tail is gas. The other is dust. As the comet moves away from the Sun, the tails shrink.

Halley's Comet is the best known periodic comet. Its first recorded sighting was in China in 240 B.C.E. It returns to Earth every 75–76 years. Its next visit to the inner solar system will be in the summer of 2061.

A comet's tail can be millions of miles long.

An asteroid called Ida has its own moon. The moon is called Dactyl.

Did You Know?

Halley's Comet last passed through Earth's atmosphere in 1986.

Are NEOs a Threat to Earth?

Near-Earth-Objects (NEOs) are small objects in the solar system. They have struck Earth in the past. They will definitely hit again. But are we in danger?

Earth has been hit by asteroids, comets, and meteorites in the past. Some scientists believe that a large asteroid collided with Central America 65 million years ago. They believe this caused the extinction of the dinosaurs. The collision created a cloud of water and rock. This material hid the Sun and covered the Earth in darkness for months or longer. Dinosaurs could not survive in the cooler climate.

Most meteors are tiny. They burn up in the Earth's atmosphere. Even those that do get through as meteorites are mostly very small. The Earth's atmosphere protects us from all objects up to about 30 feet across.

Asteroids pose a much bigger threat to Earth. This is because they tend to be much larger objects. If an asteroid with a diameter of more than a mile hit the Earth, it would cause a catastrophic planetary event. Many people would die as a result of the impact. The Earth would enter a long, cold winter where most crops die. The good news is that an asteroid of this size only collides with Earth about once every 100 million years.

The Spaceguard Survey scans the skies looking for dangerous NEOs. As yet, none that are on a collision course with Earth have been discovered. When a bigger object does head our way, we should have the advance warning and technology to deal with it.

Sometimes cosmic debris is left over from a passing comet. We get a meteor shower when this debris enters Earth's atmosphere.

Craters can be found in many places on Earth. They are the result of meteorites hitting the planet.

Huge asteroids collide with Earth about once every 100 million years. The asteroid that some people believe caused the extinction of dinosaurs was nine miles wide.

Astronomers look in space for asteroids or meteorites that might be headed toward Earth.

Seasons on Earth

*Earth's revolution around the Sun creates the seasons. They are different in the Northern and Southern **Hemispheres**.*

What Causes Seasons?

Earth completes a **revolution** around the Sun over 365 $\frac{1}{4}$ days. It is this orbit, combined with the tilt of Earth's axis, that causes the seasons. The tilt is approximately 23.5 degrees. This means that the Earth leans slightly toward the Sun.

The Northern Hemisphere is tilted toward the Sun for part of the year. The Sun is closer to the Northern Hemisphere during this time. This means the Northern Hemisphere is in the direct path of the Sun's energy. The Sun's rays are concentrated as they hit Earth. This is because they've traveled less distance through the atmosphere. The Sun rises higher in the sky and produces longer days. This is the Northern Hemisphere's summer.

At the same time, the Southern Hemisphere is tilted away from the Sun. The Sun's rays hit Earth at an angle. The Sun's energy is weaker because it has traveled through more of the atmosphere. The Sun doesn't rise as high in the sky and the days are shorter. This is winter in the Southern Hemisphere.

Did You Know?

When it is spring and autumn, neither hemisphere is tilted toward the Sun.

When it is summer in the Southern Hemisphere,
it is winter in the Northern Hemisphere.

In some regions of the planet, like
India, people refer to wet and dry
seasons instead of the four seasons.

Day and Night

Earth's rotation on its axis causes day and night.

Sunlight only falls on one-half of the planet as Earth spins. This means it is daytime on that side of Earth. On the other side, it is night.

The apparent movement of the Sun across the sky is actually due to the rotation of our Earth. The Sun always appears to rise in the east and set in the west. This is true regardless of where you are on Earth.

When the Sun rises, that part of the Earth is turning to face the Sun. When the Sun sets, that part of the Earth is turning away from the Sun. The Sun itself doesn't actually "rise" or "set."

Each planet spins around, or rotates, on its axis. Earth spins around at a speed of 994 miles per hour. Earth takes almost 24 hours to complete one rotation around the Sun. Because each rotation takes slightly less than 24 hours, the calendar needed adjusting. Leap years add an extra day, February 29th, to the calendar every four years so that the calendar aligns with Earth's motion around the Sun.

Moon Phases

Sunlight is reflected from the Moon's surface. We see different amounts of the Moon's sunlit face depending on the Moon's orbit and Earth's orbit. These are known as phases of the Moon.

Axis
23.5° angle

To the Sun

Elliptic

Nights on average are shorter than days. The Sun's light still reaches the ground even when the Sun has gone down. This is because of the way light passes through the atmosphere.

The Moon's surface doesn't give off any light. Instead it reflects the light of the Sun.

Phases of the Moon

Waxing Gibbous
More than one-half of the Moon is lit by direct sunlight.

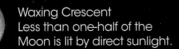

Full Moon
Two weeks after the new Moon, the Moon is halfway through its orbit. The Moon's sunlit side is facing Earth.

First Quarter
One-half of the Moon is lit by direct sunlight.

Waning Gibbous
More than one-half of the Moon is lit by direct sunlight.

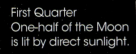

Waxing Crescent
Less than one-half of the Moon is lit by direct sunlight.

Last Quarter
One-half of the Moon is lit by direct sunlight.

New Moon
The Moon is between Earth and the Sun. The Moon's unlit side is facing Earth.

Waning Crescent
Less than one-half of the Moon is lit by direct sunlight.

Solar Eclipse

Sometimes the Moon moves between the Sun and the Earth so the three are in a straight line. The Moon blocks the Sun's light. Part of the Earth is in the Moon's shadow. This is a solar eclipse.

Discover what happens in a solar eclipse.

What You Need:

- a globe of the Earth
- a ball with string attached (Moon)
- a flashlight (Sun)

1 Place the Earth, Moon, and Sun in line so that the Moon is in the middle.

2 Turn on the Sun. Observe the shadow that falls on a small part of Earth.

3 Rotate the Earth so that the eclipse occurs where you live.

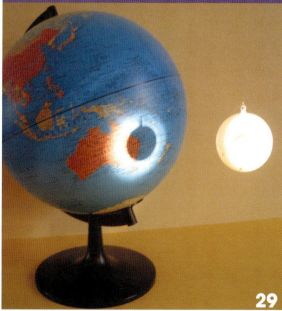

29

Space Bodies

Body	Size (compared to Earth)	Interesting Fact
Sun	332,950 x Earth	The Sun is so massive that its interior could hold 1.3 million Earths.
Mercury	0.055 x Earth	Because of its **proximity** to the Sun, the average surface temperature on Mercury is 354 degrees Fahrenheit.
Venus	0.815 x Earth	Venus was named after the Roman goddess of love and beauty. This is probably due to the fact that Venus is very bright in the night sky in comparison to the other planets.
Earth	1 x Earth	The Earth's surface is made up of 71% water. Earth is the only planet that has liquid water on its surface.
Mars	0.107 x Earth	The solar day on Mars is very close to Earth's: 24 hours, 39 minutes, and 35.244 seconds.
Jupiter	317.8 x Earth	Although Jupiter consists mainly of gas, its core is quite different. It consists of rocky material which equals roughly the mass of 10–15 Earths.
Saturn	95.162 x Earth	Because Saturn's core is so hot, it radiates more energy into space than it receives from the Sun.
Uranus	14.536 x Earth	Uranus, like Saturn, Jupiter, and Neptune, also has rings. All the rings are very faint. The outermost ring, known as Epsilon, is mostly ice boulders, several feet across.
Neptune	17.147 x Earth	Neptune has the strongest winds recorded of any planet. They can reach up to 1,200 miles per hour.

Glossary

atmospheres (AT muh sfihrs) layers of gases surrounding planets

axis (AK sihs) an imaginary line which passes through a planet, from the North to the South Pole

cores (kohrs) central parts of objects

craters (KRAY tuhrs) hollow dips resulting from the collision of an object with a planet

debris (duh BREE) scattered fragments

dwarf star (dwawrf stahr) a smaller-sized star (our Sun is a yellow dwarf star)

elliptical (ih LIHP tuh kuhl) the shape of an oval

gamma rays (GAM uh rays) high-energy waves that come from a radioactive source

gravity (GRAV uh tee) the force that attracts all bodies in the Universe to each other

greenhouse effect (GREEN hows uh FEHKT) the heating that occurs when gases trap heat and stop it from escaping a planet's atmosphere

hemispheres (HEHM uh sfihrs) the northern and southern halves of Earth

Kuiper Belt (KY puhr behlt) a disk-shaped region of minor planets and ice outside the orbit of Neptune

mass (mas) the amount of matter in an object

meteorites (MEE tee uh ryts) pieces of metal or stone from outer space that have reached Earth

nuclear reactions (NOO klee uhr ree AK shuhns) collisions of atoms giving off energy

orbit (AWR biht) the path that an object makes around another object

proximity (prok SIHM uh tee) closeness between two objects

radiates (RAY dee aytz) gives off heat or light

radiation (RAY dee AY shuhn) the release of energy in the form of waves or rays

revolution (REHV uh LOO shuhn) the movement of a heavenly body in an orbit around another heavenly body

rotation (roh TAY shuhn) turning round and round, like a wheel

satellites (SAT uh lyts) objects that revolve around a planet

sulfuric acid (suhl FYUR ihk AS ihd) a strong mineral acid

surface (SUR fihs) the outside of anything

ultraviolet (UHL truh VY uh liht) invisible rays in sunlight

waning (WAY nihng) getting smaller

water ice (WAWT uhr ys) water frozen in the solid state

waxing (WAK sihng) getting bigger

Index